In the Big Box

Written by Hawys Morgan
Photographed by Will Amlot

Collins

This tin van is quick.

The ships will not sink.

wet

This big jet hangs up.

wing

Ted has a velvet jacket.

jug

cup

9

This wax doll has socks.

box

I chat and hug my doll.

rag doll

/x/

14

/th/

After reading

Letters and Sounds: Phase 3

Word count: 39

Focus phonemes: /j/ /v/ /w/ /x/ /qu/ /ch/ /sh/ /th/ /ng/ /nk/

Common exception words: the, I, my

Curriculum links: Understanding the World: People and communities

Early learning goals: Reading: use phonic knowledge to decode regular words and read them aloud accurately, read some common irregular words, demonstrate understanding when talking with others about what they have read

Developing fluency

- Your child may enjoy hearing you read the book.
- You could take turns to read pages with lots of expression, pointing out the objects as you read.

Phonic practice

- Look at page 3. Ask your child to point to the word **pink**. Together, sound talk and blend it: p/i/nk.
- Ask your child if they can find another word with the /nk/ sound (page 4 – *sink*). Ask your child to sound talk and blend it.
- Can your child think of any other words with the /nk/ sound? (e.g. *think, rink, link*)
- Now look at "I spy sounds" on pages 14 to 15. How many words can your child spot that have the /x/ sound in them (*saxophone, fox, box*) or the /th/ sound in them? (*sloth, teeth, feather*)

Extending vocabulary

- Ask your child to find the odd one out in each of the following groups of words (you may wish to read them to your child):

think	hug	cuddle	(*think*)
talk	doll	chat	(*doll*)
quick	fast	sink	(*sink*)
legs	jacket	coat	(*legs*)